WHY IS IT HARD
to find a Job after 50?

We aren't dead yet!

Don Wicker, Ph.D.

authorHOUSE®

AuthorHouse™
1663 Liberty Drive
Bloomington, IN 47403
www.authorhouse.com
Phone: 1-800-839-8640

Published by AuthorHouse 10/23/2013

ISBN: 978-1-4918-2996-7 (sc)
ISBN: 978-1-4918-2995-0 (e)

Library of Congress Control Number: 2013919089

Any people depicted in stock imagery provided by Thinkstock are models, and such images are being used for illustrative purposes only. Certain stock imagery © Thinkstock.

This book is printed on acid-free paper.

About the Author

Dr. Don Wicker is a professor of business and management at Brazosport College in Lake Jackson, Texas. He holds a doctoral degree in organization and management with a concentration in leadership. He teaches at the undergraduate and graduate levels, and he has published six books. He has held visiting posts at universities throughout Michigan and Texas since 1999.

Other books Dr. Wicker has authored include *Goal Setting*, *Motivation: An Interactive Guide*, *Attitude Is #1*, *Job Satisfaction*, and *Success Is for Everyone*.

During his twenty-one-year career in business with General Motors Corporation, Dr. Wicker was a senior manager in the areas and departments of accounting, auditing, finance, vehicle sales, service, and marketing.

Acknowledgments

To Mary Wicker, my wife and best friend, thanks for your continued support during this very important project. To the countless people that were willing to discuss this issue with me for the past year, thanks for your support. Finally, I would like to thank all of the college professors that added suggestions and comments to this book.

Contents

Introduction

Why is it hard to find a job after fifty? In this book we will investigate reasons and theories of why it is difficult to find employment after fifty years of age. We will review the attitudes and perceptions of older workers. Do most people believe that older workers are an asset to their organizations? It appears that some older employees are made to feel as if their usefulness has passed them by. Some are patronized by younger staff and made to feel like outsiders in their own departments. Are older workers and prospective employees discriminated against? These and other questions will be analyzed in detail. Looking closer at the hiring process will assist in helping the prospective employee find employment. Although many factors are involved in the hiring process, we will start with the basics, such as the all-inclusive résumé. Your résumé could be telling an employer that you were fired from your last job because of age.

It is time to take responsibility for your life. Do you enjoy working alone on a project, or do you prefer having other people involved? Does working as part of a team improve your work, or does it interfere with your concentration? Do you feel self-confident when you are at work? It is time to change your life. If you are reading this book, obviously you have determined that age is a factor when searching for a job. Finding a job is never easy; however, it becomes extremely difficult at age fifty. After reading this book you will develop a plan of action that will assist you in finding employment after age fifty.

At the end of each chapter, you are asked to take an interactive approach to your own needs and desires by developing an action plan to assist in improving your chances. I take comfort in the fact that readers are analyzing their lives; however, I want all readers of this book to take action and develop a plan to obtain employment after fifty.

As most people know, an action plan is a document that lists steps to achieve a specific goal. The purpose of an action plan is to clarify what resources are required to reach a goal, formulate timelines for specific tasks, and determine what resources are required.

A good action plan sets the stage for achieving goals; it maps out the work process with detailed scheduling of key activities needed to accomplish specific tasks. When writing a plan of action, make sure to include the following points.

- Clarify your goals. What does the expected outcome look like?
  How will you know if you have reached your destination?

What makes your goal measurable?
What constraints do you have, such as limits on time, money, or other resources?

- Write a list of actions. Write down all actions you may need to take to achieve goals. Write as many different options and ideas as possible. Take a sheet of paper and write more and more ideas, just as they come to your mind.

- Analyze, prioritize, and frame. Look at your list of actions. What are the absolutely necessary and effective steps to achieve goals?
  Then determine what action items can be dropped from the plan without significant consequences for the outcome.

- Organize your list into a plan. Decide on the order of your action steps. Start by looking at your marked key actions. For each action, what other steps should be completed before that action? Rearrange your actions and ideas into a sequence of ordered action steps. Finally, look at your plan once again; are there any ways to simplify it even more?

Monitor the execution of your plan to measure for success. How much have you progressed toward your goal by now? One important thing to do that I described in a previous book is to record your goals and steps. On a separate sheet of paper, write down just ten things that you would like to accomplish this year.

You may be asking yourself questions at this point, such as, what are plans and goals? These are future outcomes that individuals and groups desire and strive to achieve. What is goal setting? The goal-setting process is one of the most unique and important motivational tools for effecting the performance of an individual.

There are five basic reasons goals are important.

1. Goals guide and direct behavior.
2. Goals provide challenges.
3. Goals justify the performance.
4. Goals define the basis for strategy.
5. Goals serve an organizing function.

In *Webster's Dictionary*, a goal is defined as the place at which a race, or a trip, has ended, an end that one strives to attain, the place over or into which the ball or puck must go to score. In the twenty-first century, a goal is considered the process of specifying the final and desired outcomes. In a more traditional way, a goal is defined as a process of deciding specific targets that are usually time bound, measurable, and realistic. It commonly involves:

- the end points we want to reach;
- the action plan to reach them;
- deadlines (time limit to achieve the goal).

Some traditionalists describe goal setting using the simple acronym SMART, which stands for:

Specific: clearly defined or identified
Measurable: measured perceptibly or significantly
Attainable: can be gained as an objective
Realistic: expressing an awareness of things as they really are
Time bound: in the measured or measurable period

Personally, I define goal setting on a totally new level. If you are interested, continue reading about this wonderful process. I have come to the conclusion that I don't think of goal setting as a technique. It is a natural process of forming goals in the mind. It is the process with which we move forward in time and keep reaching somewhere. Therefore, goals are not only the final destination but also the stepping stones for a much bigger outcome. They act as our direction arrows. I like to think of goal setting in two ways: *conscious* goal setting and *unconscious* goal setting.

We are mostly interested in conscious goal setting. Conscious goal setting is what most people are aware of. It is the essential element in all big achievements, and it demands attention and willpower. It basically means deciding your goals in advance, consciously and in a proper manner, instead of just going with the flow, instead of with whatever your conditioning is doing to you. Although behavioral science recognizes that people can skillfully pursue goals without consciously attending to their behavior once these goals are set, conscious will is considered to be the starting point of goal pursuit. Indeed, when we decide to work hard on a task, it feels as if that conscious decision is the first and foremost cause of our behavior.

older people lose the ability to see as well as they did in their younger days. Also, their reflexes are not as quick as they once were. Therefore, driving could be a dangerous task. Some of these family members are in their fifties, sixties, or seventies; can you imagine taking away someone's ability to drive simply because they are too old?

Do these actions alter our perception of older workers? For example, imagine you are a manager with older parents that needed to stop driving due to their advancing age and for safety reasons, and they are sixty. Do you think that might have an effect on your views of older workers? Say, for instance, it is time to assign important projects to one of your coordinators at work. One of them happens to be thirty, and the other happens to be sixty. Remember, you just stopped your parent from driving at age sixty, and now you have an important project to assign that could possibly go to the older worker. It is easy to say that your perception about older workers should not be altered. However, our perception can be altered based on experience, because perception depends on how the perceiver interprets sensory stimuli, although we know errors or misperceptions are bound to occur. For example, have you ever been in the driver's seat when the car next to you begins to back up, and you think your car is going to move forward? When that happens to me, I slam on my brakes before realizing that I have just experienced a perceptual illusion called induced movement. My mind told me something was going to happen; however, nothing did. It was as if my mind was playing tricks on me.

Where do our perceptions regarding age come from? Let's analyze the aging process. It is the progressive deterioration of the body that culminates in death. People can age in at least two ways, chronologically and functionally. Your chronological age is the number of years you have lived, while your functional age is a measure of how well you can physically and mentally function in your surroundings. Chronological age and functional age are not always in harmony. For example, some fifty-five-year olds function like a typical thirty-five-year old, while other fifty-five-year-olds function like a typical sixty-five-year-old. When a person reaches his or her twenties, the body operates at peak performance. However, when a person reaches his or her thirties or forties, outward signs of aging become more noticeable. Hair thins and turns gray, wrinkles develop, and vision declines. By age seventy bone compression in the spinal column causes changes in posture, and people have shrunk one to two inches.

All of these factors play a role in our perception of people over fifty. A study by Selkoe (1992) revealed significant changes in the brain as we age. After age fifty, people begin losing neurons at an accelerated rate, so that at death people may have about 5 percent less brain mass than they had in young adulthood.

The good news is that the increasing number of older workers may break down barriers and prejudices.

Asking an economist if it is a good thing that older people are working more is like asking a vegetarian about the falling price of beef. Eroding pensions, 401(k) assets in mutual funds declining by 40 percent in years past, and a lousy economy explain why many older people are clinging to their jobs or returning to the labor market after retiring.

A hidden cause of the increase in age discrimination claims is the pension crisis. Everyone who wants to work should be able to, and no one deserves to be judged by age or any other factor that does not relate to his or her productivity. Forcing older people to work to cover their pension losses will have the unintended effect of causing more age discrimination claims in the workplace.

Plan of Action

List the steps you are going to take to stay current and engaged with society regarding your perception of older workers.

_____

_____

_____

_____

_____

_____

_____

_____

_____

_____

_____

_____

_____

_____

_____

_____

_____

_____

_____

_____

_____

_____

What Does It Take to Be an Entrepreneur?

Here are some of the main characteristics of a successful entrepreneur.

- Self-directed: directed or guided by oneself, especially as an independent
- Self-nurturing: takes care of oneself, valuing one's own well-being
- Action-oriented: performs work with energy and drive; values planning
- Highly energetic: displays energy, especially in abundance
- Tolerant of uncertainty: inclined to tolerate the beliefs of others

These are all fantastic qualities to possess; however, I believe one quality is almost always overlooked. That quality is experience. Who are the most experienced workers? Older people. Yes, older people usually have the most experience, in business and in other areas of life. When you are talking about the operation of a business, experience is the key ingredient for success. It is sort of like baking a cake. To bake a delicious cake you need several different key ingredients such as; sugar, flour, eggs, frosting, and a variety of other things. To operate a business successfully, you need to be self-directed, self-nurturing, action-oriented, highly energetic, tolerant of uncertainty, and—the key ingredient— experienced.

Pursuing a career as an entrepreneur is not easy. There is work involved, it can be stressful, and you may not always be successful. People seem to learn from their failures. Sometimes failure needs to be experienced to set oneself up for a more successful future as an entrepreneur. A setback could be a setup for a comeback.

When you end up making money and creating an impact on society, everything leading up to your success will have been worth it. Be creative; sometimes the most successful entrepreneur is not the one that comes up with an idea first, but the one that executes it more creatively.

Almost anything we think of has already been thought of or created by someone else, which has never stopped successful entrepreneurs. When the movie rental business was going through market changes, Redbox and Netflix were created with an innovative way of providing a more affordable and convenient automated movie rental service. Like Steve Jobs, who was a visionary ahead of his time, successful entrepreneurs have the gift to see beyond their current circumstances. They can see opportunities where everybody else sees problems, chaos, and confusion.

It is their ability to envision a better tomorrow that guides them toward success.

Successful entrepreneurs have the courage to do what most people would not, despite circumstances. Successful entrepreneurs may fear failure, but their fears don't stop them from doing what they think is correct to achieve their goals. They would rather say "can't do it" if things don't go well, instead of "what if?" They are willing to take risks for better or for worse.

Plan of Action

List the steps you are going to take to become a successful entrepreneur.

_____

_____

_____

_____

_____

_____

_____

_____

Why is it hard to find a Job after 50?

When Does Age Discrimination Start?

Age discrimination has been illegal in the United States since 1967. I am not saying that age discrimination does not exist; however, it is in a more restrained form. About 80 percent of executives believe there is moderate or severe age discrimination in the workplace. According to a recent survey of nine hundred senior-level executives age forty or older, they believe job opportunities have been lost because of age.

At what point does age begin to affect hiring decisions negatively?

Percentages of senior-level executives who said hiring decisions were affected negatively by age are shown below.

Employees -

Before age 50 – senior level Executives said hiring decision were affected 24%.

Between age 50 and 54 – senior level Executives said hiring decision were affected 39%.

Between ages 55 and 59 – senior level Executives said hiring decision were affected 23%.

Age 60 and older – senior level Executives said hiring decision were affected 11%.

The senior-level executives clearly illustrate that age can negatively affect hiring decisions.

People between forty and eighty seem to have better emotions and mind-sets. A study by D. Watson, published by the Guilford Press (2000), revealed that people ages 18 to 94 negative emotions seem to occur less as people get older. Therefore, the older you get, the less negative emotions you will have. The study also revealed periods of highly positive moods lasted longer for older individuals, and bad moods faded more quickly. The study implies that emotional experience improves with age; as we get older, we experience fewer negative emotions. Wouldn't that imply that older people would be good employment candidates?

Plan of Action

List the steps you plan on taking to eliminate age discrimination.

_____

_____

_____

_____

Don Wicker, Ph.D.

Does Your Résumé Look Outdated?

Your résumé could be telling an employer that you were let go because of age. If your previous job responsibility is higher than the job you are applying for, that could be a red flag, depending on your age. Remember, people in mid-career do not quit their jobs without having another one firmly in hand. Look at your own résumé. One job follows another, usually without a break.

Don't sell yourself short or let misinterpretations get you down. You have experience, both work experience and real-life experience, which indicates that you have real assets. The human side of any organization is even more important. Human nature does not really change, and experience is forever valued. The human side of you is your years of work experience.

I think back to my days in corporate America, and I can remember coworkers always speaking of retiring. During this period of time, most workers expected to work twenty, thirty, or forty years with the same company. Most people I knew that worked for General Motors Corporation never thought about searching for new employment when they reached fifty or sixty years of age. Unfortunately, the time has come that unemployment at these ages is not unusual. Employees with decades of work experience, numerous corporate training classes, one or two college degrees, and out of work. What a travesty.

Wait one second: my last description of an employee is not bad. So why can't someone with years of experience and one or two college degrees find employment? Could it be a faulty résumé?

When communicating your résumé in writing, exclude certain sections of information. For instance, try not to disclose the years in which you accomplished certain tasks. Never disclose the years in which you graduated from high school, college, or any other school. Try not to identify by date when you obtained your first job. You can always discuss these very important dates at another time. The task is to avoid getting eliminated in the initial screening. It is fairly easy to articulate yourself in a face-to-face meeting, demonstrating your skills and youthful ideals. However, disclosing certain time frames could have your résumé eliminated before the process starts.

Can work have an impact on success or failure for an individual? When we think of working, we sometimes think of how job satisfaction is related to success. Job satisfaction can have a profound effect on how we view work and success in our lives. When we talk about job satisfaction, what do we mean? One definition of job satisfaction calls it "a sense of inner fulfillment and pride achieved when performing a particular job" (Webster, 2010). Job satisfaction occurs when an employee feels he or she has accomplished something having importance and value worth recognition.

To the worker job satisfaction brings a pleasurable emotional state that often leads to a positive work attitude and improved performance. A satisfied worker is more likely to be creative, flexible, innovative, and loyal. The behaviorist Abraham Maslow said that to be truly satisfied with our lives and career, we must fully use our natural aptitudes and skills (Maslow, 1991). Does this sound like you? Can you say that your job or career gives you complete satisfaction? Has your performance improved because of job satisfaction?

I have a friend who works in management for a chemical company, where he manages the shipping department. His responsibilities and stress are average, meaning that he has very few sleepless nights related to work. He often works very hard to achieve his work objectives. I often ask him if he is satisfied with his career and his job. The response I usually receive from him is, "It pays the bills." When my friend replies that his job simply pays the bills, I realize that this is a big indicator that job satisfaction is absent from his life. How can a person be satisfied in a job if it serves only one purpose, namely, to pay the bills? What happens when a job or career cannot serve any purpose? What happens when bills outweigh the weekly paycheck? If the job that a person relies on for support cannot pay the bills, the worker has no source of job satisfaction. The job becomes a routine task that must be completed day after day, forever.

As many people know, most employees pretend to be satisfied with their jobs. They may tell their boss, friends, and coworkers that they are satisfied with their jobs. However, when we analyze the behavior of those individuals, it is very easy to see that they are engaging in a daily activity that is not enjoyable. A simple test to determine if someone is satisfied with his or her job is to observe that individual's passion for the job. Is the passion genuine or fake? If you ask people, "If you won 50 million dollars, would you continue to work?" most individuals who experience total job satisfaction would respond with a definite yes! Think about it: can you honestly say you would work for free or that if you won a large sum of money you would continue working? I honestly can say I am one of those people. Yes, even if I won 50 million dollars and could afford not to concern myself about money again, I would work—not just to have somewhere to go each day, but to experience total job satisfaction every day that I go to work. I must say it is an awesome feeling to experience enjoyment on a daily basis! Working tirelessly at something enjoyable day after day is a feeling that everyone should experience at some point in his or her life. Why live life any other way?

Job satisfaction should make people feel like they need to pay their employer for allowing them to work. I know that is an extreme statement; however, that is the passion and enjoyment people should feel for their work every day. Most people who have experienced true job satisfaction will state, "My occupation does not feel like work." Alternatively, as some people say, "If you love your work, you will never work a day in your life."

Plan of Action

List the steps you are going to take to improve the appearance of your résumé.

_____

_____

_____

_____

_____

_____

_____

_____

_____

_____

_____

_____

Don Wicker, Ph.D.

_____

_____

_____

_____

_____

_____

_____

_____

_____

_____

_____

_____

_____

_____

_____

_____

_____

_____

_____

_____

Taking Responsibility for Your Life

Do you enjoy working alone on a project, or do you prefer having other people involved? Does working as part of a team improve your work, or does it interfere with your concentration?

Do you feel self-confident when you are at work? Does it seem to you that you are doing a good job and that other people know it? Are you in the network? In other words, do you know what is going on, and do you play an important role in advancing your organization's goals?

How do you define success? Do you want a job that you love or a paycheck that satisfies you? In a tough economy where jobs are scarce, many of us believe that we must, to some degree, choose between one and the other. The reality is that lack of money is one of the top causes of stress in the United States. The American Psychological Association's most recent annual Stress in America report found that 75 percent of those surveyed said money was a significant source of stress in their lives, while another 70 percent cited work as causing major stress (APA, 2012). It is only natural that in this circumstance we feel forced to choose between love and money. Normally we panic and choose money.

As a result, many of us end up in jobs we dislike or in careers to which we are not well matched. It comes as no surprise that some statistics state that up to 80 percent of employees dislike their jobs! Yet employees spend more of their lives working than doing just about anything else. Being miserable at work is certainly no measure of success, regardless of the paycheck in your pocket. It will not happen overnight, but with thoughtful planning you can obtain any opportunity that you desire. All it takes is for you to get serious and develop a plan to succeed.

Developing a plan to succeed is as simple as determining what you enjoy doing. It is up to each individual to find their true calling in life. Success comes from working hard, with purpose, focus, discipline, and persistence. To make your efforts the most effective, put together a plan. To get where you choose to go, you must know clearly where that is. The more precisely you can envision and anticipate the steps along the way, the more successful you will be. There are many factors working against you when taking each step along the path to success. One powerful way to facilitate taking the next step is to know precisely what it is. When you have a good, solid plan, the distractions are not as distracting. When you are following your plan, you can more quickly recover from setbacks. Your plan keeps you focused on and connected with your purpose. Having a plan enables you to build powerful, positive momentum in your efforts. Anything that is worth doing is also worth the time and effort spent to establish a workable plan. Plan to succeed and you will.

Plan of Action

List the steps you are going to take regarding your personal plan of action to succeed.

_____

_____

_____

_____

_____

_____

_____

_____

_____

_____

Don Wicker, Ph.D.

Example of a University Meeting

While sitting and waiting for my meeting to start, I briefly scanned the room; it was filled with approximately five hundred adjunct faculty members. I noticed one common characteristic of these faculty members. The majority of attendees had gray hair, meaning that they were middle-aged or older. Let me clarify my last statement; it appeared that the majority of the audience was over fifty. It appears that these older, experienced adjunct or part-time professors have realized that their work experience and knowledge is a very marketable tool that can assist colleges and universities.

I am not sure if most of the college adjunct professors had intentions of teaching as they gained more work experience and knowledge; however, they have found a real niche for workers over fifty. It is amazing to talk to some of these individuals, with their diverse backgrounds and knowledge—individuals with twenty to forty years' experience in banking, automotive management, project management, strategic management, and finance, to name a few. Therefore, why not utilize their knowledge and experience to earn an income?

As technology continues to explode, educational institutions are rapidly moving toward expanding their course offerings. Most colleges and universities have recognized that using part-time or adjunct professors is a real money maker. Colleges can hire adjuncts without any risks or obligation. These professors are temporary contractors that are nonemployees. There is no obligation by the employer to continue employment, or to offer any type of benefits or perks.

The stereotype that all college faculty are full-time researchers may no longer be true. Research on part-time and non-tenure-track faculty indicates that nearly 70 percent of instructional faculty at colleges and universities now are either part-time adjunct faculty or non-tenure-track faculty.

Often, adjunct faculty members are hired because of their professional experience or to fill a need spurred by surging enrollment. People working in a specific field, such as interior design, may teach courses that explain a new technology in light design. They must meet the minimum qualifications required of a tenured or full-time faculty member, which in many cases means a master's degree or a PhD. Also, adjunct professors typically spend their entire time teaching students, which is the opposite of a tenured professor. They are not expected to conduct research, publish papers, or attend staff meetings and events, as required of tenured professors. Adjunct professors generally share offices with other adjuncts, if they have offices at all.

Plan of Action

List the steps you are going to take to become an adjunct professor, instructor, or teacher.

_____

_____

_____

_____

_____

_____

_____

_____

_____

_____

_____

_____

_____

Jobs for Workers Fifty and Over

As I sit in my local coffee shop, I ponder what happens to the worker in his or her fifties, sixties, or seventies. Should this be an age of discovery? One would think that all job or career questions would be answered; unfortunately, there is no certainty in this area. From what I observe in my local coffee shop, a dynamic community is interacting as I write. I see young people talking and networking, making those ever-important human connections. I hear young people talking about their jobs and company opportunities.

I also see high school students meeting and greeting their friends and sharing the latest conversations on their iPhones. Wait a minute. One group is noticeably absent here: individuals past fifty. Of the eighty people talking, drinking coffee, and networking, I see only four older individuals. It appears that this group is left out of utilizing this networking opportunity.

Why aren't older workers engaged in this social networking opportunity? No one can say it is because they do not need jobs. We know that people aged fifty to eighty need employment as much or maybe more than the next guy. Could pride be preventing them from making the necessary networking connections?

Another interesting observation that I happened to make while surveying the room was that most conversations were about starting businesses. I find that ironic—young people with limited experience and knowledge discussing ways to start a business, whereas older workers with years of experience and a wealth of knowledge and education are looking for jobs on the internet or in the newspapers.

Well, it is time someone informed these older individuals that they have what it takes to start a business and gain new opportunities. Get up off your old ass, and utilize your talents! No one can tell me that workers from fifty to eighty have not learned something from being in the workforce all of those years. If they worked in such jobs as paying invoices in accounts payable, they should have gained enough experience and knowledge to start an invoicing or accounts payable business. It is a fact that the average individual in this age category has a minimum of fifteen years of work experience. With that much work experience, and exceptional training, most people could start a business today. I cannot understand why older individuals will not consider starting a business. As I stated earlier, it really does not matter what type of business you were in previously. Just survey your own experience to find out what you were or are good at doing, and determine or investigate how you can make money doing it.

A human resource manager could become an HR consultant for other companies that are similar to their previous employer. A janitor could utilize his years of experience to start a cleaning company. A grade school teacher could start her own tutoring business and still have an impact on developing children's lives. A corporate accountant could start her or his own accounting firm, offering full accounting services that most companies need.

As you have read, all sorts of businesses can be created based on your work experience; however, you must be confident and have high self-discipline to start your own business. And if you are going to start a business, you must ensure that it is a business that you will enjoy, as well as having several years of experience in. For example, if you are an airline pilot with years of flying and teaching experience, the last thing you would want to do is start a trucking company because someone told you that the money was good. Doing something that you are good at and enjoy is a much better proposition.

Following the money will not make most people happy. Studies have estimated that 80 percent of workers do not like their jobs. Some jobs are high-paying, and some are low-paying, but the main point is that most people do not like their jobs. In one of my earlier books I describe a scenario where an airline pilot started a trucking company, which was not in his area of expertise. To make a long story short, the trucking company was not successful, due to his lack of experience. It would be more logical for a pilot to start his own flying school or packaging company where he is flying cargo from one location to another. Benefiting from years of flying experience would seem a logical choice; starting a business in which a person has no experience is not a smart prospect.

Possible Jobs

For your own reference, make a list of the jobs you think someone over fifty - should apply for.

_____

_____

_____

_____

_____

_____

_____

_____

_____

_____

One very interesting thing that I have observed is older people working in real estate. During the past thirty years, I have had the opportunity to purchase ten houses, and I have sold nine. I have lived in three different states and have always felt comfortable using Realtors that were older and more experienced. Most of the successful Realtors I know are older people with years of real estate experience. I have talked to numerous individuals that feel the same way I do regarding Realtors. They also believed that an older Realtor appears more credible, knowledgeable, and honest. I have always felt a real connection with older car dealers, older Realtors, and older business people. As most people say, with age comes wisdom and knowledge. I believe that people in their fifties and sixties have a real advantage in the areas I just mentioned. Let me rephrase that last statement: in the job areas I just mentioned, older people have a distinct advantage over younger people.

According to the Bureau of Labor and Statistics, the projected labor growth for seniors from 2006 to 2016 is increasing at a fast rate.

- The total number of active workers between the age of 55 and 64 will increase by 36.5%.
- The senior's labor force in the 65–74 age group is expected to rise by 83.4%.
- The anticipated growth in the number of working men and women over age 75 is a whopping 84.3%. It appears that the numbers for seniors

working will continue to increase (Monthly Labor Review, 2007).

If job loss or retirement hasn't happened to you, look out! It could be coming. Develop your detailed plan to generate income. It could be as simple as becoming a hair stylist at a salon. It's something to think about; they are popular with many, maybe even yourself. Why not try and turn something you have experienced over the years into a money-making opportunity? To continue with this example, what's really required to become a hair stylist? My research has uncovered a simple process. Enroll in hair styling classes, gain experience in a hair salon, and complete a test successfully to obtain a license. A hair stylist license gives a person the needed credibility, legal right, and confidence to work in a hair salon. A hair stylist can also obtain his or her own clients as an independent hair stylist to earn additional income. It will be income that you control; no one can determine your earning potential but you.

It is the same principle for other occupations in the service sector: manicurists, massage therapists, etc. All it takes to be successful is to really think about what your likes and dislikes are. Once you determine your likes, investigate them to determine if you can make money doing them.

Plan of Action

What is your action plan to discover jobs and opportunities that you can perform after age fifty?

_____

_____

_____

_____

_____

_____

_____

_____

_____

_____

_____

_____

Staying Home and Working

Working at home could be your next job. I believe most people would enjoy staying at home sleeping late every morning. Keeping their pajamas on all day and starting work while drinking a cup of coffee. It can be as easy as starting a company like "chefsline. com." Chefsline.com will connect cooks with advice. If an individual does not have time to read a cookbook, he or she can call or search online for chefsline.com to get advice regarding any type of food they would like to prepare. It's like having a personal cookbook. A company like this is at the crossroads of connecting at-home cooks who want instant advice, and are willing to pay for it, with experts willing to dispense advice from the home while getting paid to do so.

In the twenty-first century, companies are already discussing ways to keep the brain power of baby boomers on the payroll, either by rehiring them as consultants, where they set their own schedules, or letting them work part-time. Therefore, why not develop a way to perform your current job from home? Remember, it does not cost anything to think of ways to work from home. Give this idea some thought; maybe it can work for you.

What are the ways to determine whether you can work from home? The first thing to do would be to ask your boss. If you are working and satisfied with your job but not its location, this could be your easiest path to working from home. All you have to do is convince your boss that you can be just as effective, maybe even more so, working from your spare bedroom as your second-floor cubicle.

Many employers are looking for individuals who can work from home—people to answer calls, provide customer service, give technical assistance, or perform virtual office tasks, such as handling administrative duties. There are companies, law firms, government agencies and nonprofit organizations that are willing to set workers up at home—just ask.

Plan of Action

Make a list of jobs you can perform from your home.

_____

_____

_____

_____

_____

_____

_____

_____

_____

_____

_____

_____

_____

_____

_____

_____

_____

_____

_____

_____

_____

_____

_____

_____

Becoming a Customer Service Employee

What is customer service, and what are the requirements? As many people know, good customer service is the lifeblood of any business. One can offer promotions and slash prices to bring in as many new customers as possible, but unless one can get some of those customers to come back, the business will not be profitable for long.

Good customer service is all about bringing customers back, and who better to perform this service than a senior person with real-world wisdom? Remember, customer service is the provision of service to customers before, during, and after a purchase. According to Turban et al. (2002), customer service is a series of activities designed to enhance the level of customer satisfaction, the feeling that a product or service has met customer expectations. Depending on the service or product, most seniors would be a perfect match for these occupations. A good example of a wiser, older customer service representative helping me occurred at Home Depot. I was working on my home, trying to improve the appearance of a light fixture. I took a short trip to Home Depot and did not have an idea of where to look. However, as an older, wiser customer service representative approached me and started asking questions about my project, I felt a sense of relief. My relief occurred because of the confidence this customer service worker showed me. This customer service representative informed me of the countless times he had completed the same project in his home. With his knowledge and experience, I thought to myself, this is the perfect job for older adults. When a person can relate their past experiences and knowledge to customers, it gives a sense of confidence and relief. I truly believe that the position of customer service representative is another perfect fit for older individuals.

The best customer service representatives focus on people. They are good listeners, good communicators, and convey to us a positive and patient demeanor. These amazingly reliable people provide business owners with the competitive advantage. It does not matter if the economy is slow; successful organizations continue to recognize the importance of their employees.

Anyone considering a career in customer service must be able to handle stress and pressure, maintain friendly interactions with customers, and follow through on tasks. It is not always easy to maintain one's focus on serving people; therefore, an employer needs to identify and invest in the right people for the job, and I believe the right people are older, wiser people.

Plan of Action

List the characteristics you think are necessary to work in customer service.

_____

_____

_____

_____

_____

_____

_____

_____

_____

_____

_____

_____

_____

_____

Becoming a Cook

My aunt was born and raised in the South; however, she moved to Michigan during her adulthood. She learned how to cook from her mother and grandmother. During my aunt's lifetime, cooking was a valued skill that most people enjoyed. Her cooking skills were comparable to those of a very experienced chef. My aunt practiced those skills for forty years. She could cook any type of meal the same as that which would be prepared by a master chef in a restaurant.

Imagine: a cook that does not work in a restaurant but prepares meals and desserts as if she worked in one. I am sure my aunt was not unique; many others have the same abilities and skills. Let's examine these skills for a moment, the ability to prepare meals and desserts equivalent to a master chef. Sounds like a wonderful skill that can be turned into a profitable opportunity, turning your cooking skills into a money-generating venture. Ask people in your church or social organizations to purchase meals or desserts from you. Develop a dessert list with meals and dessert descriptions with prices. It should be easy to obtain clients, due to the number of people that you associate with. I believe cooking for others is a great way to generate income because I witnessed it working for my aunt for years. My aunt baked desserts for her church friends on a weekly basis; she created a price list for the convenience of customers. She also ensured that her expenses were covered and that a profit was generated with each sale. I will never forget how my aunt's friends would call her and order their pies and cakes; it was as if they were placing an order at a nice restaurant.

My aunt's unique way of generating income could easily be utilized by people in their fifties, sixties, and seventies. The reason I mention these ages is because these are the people with the most cooking experience. Why throw away years of cooking experience, when cooking skills can be used to generate income? Cooking for others is another way that older people can create their own job opportunities.

Plan of Action

List the skills you think are necessary to become a cook.

_____

_____

_____

_____

_____

_____

_____

_____

_____

_____

_____

_____

_____

_____

_____

_____

_____

_____

_____

_____

_____

Becoming a Communications Specialist

When we talk about communication, we refer to an all-or-nothing situation. You speak the language of the hiring organization or you do not; it's that simple. Throughout your interpersonal interactions, your face communicates, especially signaling emotions. In fact, facial movements alone seem to communicate the degree of pleasantness, agreement, and sympathy a person feels. Think about this fact for a moment; facial movements may communicate at least eight emotions: happiness, surprise, fear, anger, sadness, disgust, contempt, and interest. Which one of these emotions should you display in an interview? If you want job happiness, then I think interest should be at the top of your list.

As you learned the nonverbal system of communication during your early years, facial management techniques enabled you to communicate your feelings to achieve the effect you wanted. To hide certain emotions and to emphasize others is a way of life. A feeling of happiness should always accompany a job interview. Happiness also gives you a sense of confidence. Sound confident—not pushy—using reasonably intense language, striking metaphors, and vivid details, with a voice that is neither meek nor boisterous. Own the room, stroll into meetings, and reach out to others; make suggestions without hesitation. Always show confidence in every situation, even when you are not sure of yourself.

During the initial contact, there is a kind of perceptual connection; you see, hear, or understand through reading a message. From this you form a mental and physical picture that includes gender, approximate age, beliefs and values, height, and so on. After this perception, there is usually interactional contact. Here the contact is superficial and relatively impersonal. This is the stage at which you exchange basic information that is preliminary to intense involvement ("Hello, my name is Joe"). Here you initiate intention and engage in invitational communication. The contact stage is the time of first impressions. At the contact stage in face-to-face interaction, physical appearance is especially important, because it is the characteristic most readily seen. Yet through verbal and nonverbal behaviors, qualities such as friendliness, warmth, openness, and dynamism also are revealed.

The last two important factors in effective communication to obtain or find a job are perception and self-fulfilling prophecy. Think about this: perception is the process by which you become aware of objects, events, and especially people through your senses of sight, smell, taste, touch, and hearing. Perception is an active, not a passive, process. Your perceptions result both from what exists in the outside world and from your own experiences, desires, needs and wants, loves and hatreds. Among the reasons perception is so important in interpersonal communication is that it influences your communication choices. The messages we send and listen to will depend on how we see the world, on how we size up specific situations, on what we think of people with whom we interact.

Without perception, we sometimes distort our self-fulfilling prophecy. A self-fulfilling prophecy is a prediction that comes true because we act on it as if it were true. Put differently, a self-fulfilling prophecy occurs when we act on our ideas as if they were true and in doing so we make them true. The self-fulfilling prophecy also can be seen when we make predictions about ourselves and fulfill them. For example, suppose we enter a group situation convinced that the other members will dislike us. What we may be doing is acting in a way that encourages the group to respond to us negatively; in this way we fulfill our prophecies about ourselves.

Self-fulfilling prophecies can short-circuit critical thinking and influence others behaviors to conform. As a result, we may see what we predicted rather than what is really in existence.

Plan of Action

List the behaviors and characteristics needed to become a good communicator.

_____

_____

_____

_____

_____

_____

_____

_____

_____

_____

_____

_____

_____

_____

Using Your Life Experiences to Find You

It is very important to find something you love or to analyze your past to find a job you loved in the past. Can it get easier to find a job after fifty? It should, because by the age of fifty a person should be in a position to determine what he or she loves. I think it's never too late to love your job. Whether you're re-careering, reinventing, rediscovering, or just looking to get your passion back, finding fulfillment in the workplace does not equate to starting from scratch.

A good question to ask yourself is; when was the last time you were passionate about work. When was the last time you genuinely anticipated waking up and going to work? When you determine what that is, it will be easy to turn that skill into a job that can last for years after fifty.

A majority of American workers say they're unsatisfied with their jobs, and only 15.4 percent pronounce themselves very satisfied in their work, according to a new report by a conference board on business membership and research. This group has been conducting surveys about worker happiness for years (Conference Board, 2013).

One thing is for sure: an employee can fall in love with work again even if she or he has been in a job for decades. Talk with enough happy workers, and you find that being older doesn't have to equal unhappiness. The secret is feeling in control: having a job that offers a larger say in what goes on at work, more flexibility in scheduling day-to-day activities, and more opportunities to pursue professional passions and develop new skills. It is a simple proposition: determine what you are good at, and try to make money while doing it. I'm not referring to some sort of outdated process that you learned in the first years of employment in 1980. No, I'm talking about some modern process or technique that's currently utilized in the twenty-first century. That's why it is extremely important for older workers to make sure their job skills are up-to-date, so they can keep up with younger colleagues. Also, learning can boost your mood as well as your prospects. Older workers should always challenge themselves to add skills and stretch their abilities. Taking advantage of opportunities will more than likely give confidence and shift you in a new direction. The ability to shift is needed when it is time to sell your knowledge and experience to an employer as a consultant, trainer, or salesperson.

Finally, we must remember that sometimes a job is just a job. The satisfaction comes from the add-ons, such as training, mentoring, and volunteering for projects outside the scope of responsibilities. Look more thoroughly around your organization, and see how you can get involved to help your organization and yourself. Helping yourself will allow you to identify what you enjoy most at work. Once identified, try and turn it into a money-making opportunity.

I recently encountered such an opportunity for my wife. One day my wife was showing my daughter how to play a song on our piano. My daughter learned how to play songs on the piano at school, and she wanted to demonstrate it for my wife and me. She played the song well; however, she hit a few wrong notes. My wife recognized this after she finished the song, and she began to correct the problem. My wife's musical knowledge is amazing, she can play the piano, and she has talent with regard to reading music. I began to analyze her musical history to determine her skill level. I found out that my wife studied piano throughout her childhood while growing up in her home country of the Philippines. It was only after she moved to the United States at the age of thirteen that she stopped pursuing her parents' dream of being a pianist. I did not analyze her skill level to encourage her to be a professional musician; however, I did want her to understand the knowledge and skill she had acquired in music. She started taking piano lessons at age two; therefore, she had studied the piano for eleven years. She knows how to read music, play complete songs without looking at the piano keys, and is an excellent teacher. If we explore this story further, you can began to identify an income opportunity in my wife's future.

When my wife was teaching my daughter, it was

obvious that she really enjoyed teaching. She has always enjoyed working with people, and she has a unique way of relating to young people. She is a petite woman with a bundle of energy. That is why young girls and boys seem to enjoy her company. Whatever it is, it works! I also asked my wife what would happen if she started to study music again? She stated that her skill level and knowledge of the piano would increase. My next question was a simple one, "Could you teach piano to children and young people? "Her response: "That would be fun!" Fun and enjoyment is the main premise of this book, finding something that you enjoy doing and trying to make a living doing it. I challenged my wife to continue studying piano, and also to determine which children in the area have an interest in studying piano as an after-school activity. To begin this process, she should start surveying different schools and music departments in grade school, and networking with moms, children, and afterschool programs. If my wife follows this plan during the next seven years, she will be able to retire from her current employer, provide a service to the community, and generate significant income from giving piano lessons or starting a piano school.

Trying to reinvent yourself after fifty is a simple process. Find something you enjoy or like doing, and try to make money doing it. I believe that every person over fifty should analyze their personal assets! Your background and experiences will include workplace skills you are currently using, transferable skills learned from previous employment, and life skills learned from living day to day. A few examples of life skills are the ability to edit written material, teach piano, build websites, or tutor math. There are numerous ideas and opportunities available to everyone; we just need to think about things we are good at doing.

How have you helped past employers succeed? If you were successful at something in the past (for instance, solving problems), you should be able to apply that knowledge and experience for other employers or for your own business. Focus on positive results you have obtained from previous employers. This in turn will shift the focus from your age to your abilities. A good example of workplace skills for the average worker compiled over several years could look like the following.

Examples of Job Skills

sales	analyzing data	training	assembling	presenting seminars
budgeting	creating flyers	child care	speaking	software development
writing	problem solving	coaching	mentoring	making decisions
liaison	team development	evaluating	maintenance	production planning
leading	investigating	recruiting	painting	dispensing medications

Determine your lists of job skills and experiences learned over the years. In addition to job skills, various life stages of an adult provide an accumulation of transferable and life skills that could benefit your own business venture. Skills acquired from activities you have accomplished for yourself, your family, and organizations to which you belong can transfer to a new business venture. For instance, raising your own children could give you the skills needed to provide child care at your own day care facility. Someone who provided home health care for a sick relative could provide the same kind of care to other ill individuals in their own home health care business.

Individuals must get creative when matching skills with potential entrepreneurial opportunities. I have compiled a list of transferable and life skills that employees fifty and over possess and can utilize. In the next section determine which transferable skills can assist you in generating income.

Example of Transferable Skills

customer service	handling money	teaching
filing or keeping records	cooking	demonstrating products
operating a cash register	preparing bulk mailings	maintaining appointments
bill collections	operating machines	directing workflow
landscaping	ordering supplies	ordering products

Life skills should be analyzed to determine their usefulness in generating extra income. The transferable skills listed above could be your opportunity to generate income. Simply take a long, critical look into the items described above and determine your next steps. For example, if you have been filing or keeping records organized for the past ten years at your current job, your filing and organizing skills and techniques should be more advanced than the average person's. Maybe you developed some type of neat system or technique that keeps your records in a sequential order. What if you developed this system to the point that you could sell it to other businesses? Offering your services as a file organizing expert; your task could be to help companies get organized. You accomplish this by going into a company and assisting the staff in getting organized. Most companies' filing and record-keeping systems are in total disarray; therefore, you could be labeled as the "file fixer." You visit companies to help them get organized. Develop your process and start selling your services; it's that easy!

Example of Life Skills

maintain personal web-site	scheduler	fund-raising
party planning	planning sports	coaching
tax return preparation	repairing	buying goods
paying bills	cooking	cleaning
child care	budget preparation	exercising

Try to obtain positive personal characteristics to enhance your ability to generate extra income. It is not too late; start today to acquire some of the skills listed below.

Examples of Personal Characteristics

energetic	visionary	thinks critically	dependable
tech-certified	coaching	innovative	logical
positive attitude	open-minded	flexible	progressive
motivated	positive	loyal	honest

Hopefully, the previous lists provided assistance in determining what you enjoy or like doing. Again, I must say once you determine what you enjoy or like, try to turn it into a permanent income to sustain you and your family.

My own sister has transferable skills that could be turned into a business or money-making opportunity. She has been teaching elementary school in the Pontiac, Michigan, school district for over twenty-eight years. She has obtained thousands of hours of training, teaching, certifications, experience, and seminars to improve her skills as a teacher. Having spent a lifetime trying to form and improve the minds of elementary school students, it is all she knows and enjoys.

Years ago I informed her that she has been given a golden opportunity to generate income after she retires. With her teaching experience and knowledge, she should be working to set up her own tutoring or teacher training consulting business. The best type of trainer is someone that has been in the field for over a decade. Networking her skills to other school districts would be a natural fit. Developing a system to train teachers as she was trained over the past decade would be a fairly simple process.

After all, she understands how training has worked in the past; she also understands what training has not worked best with teachers during her tenure. The opportunity for my sister would be to start her own consulting firm that would offer training to teachers.

Another area of my sister's experience that could be used to start a business or generate income would be her teaching. She has experience teaching hundreds of subjects to a wide range of different ages of students. She understands their learning patterns and study habits. Therefore, she could develop a tutoring program to improve student knowledge. It is never too late to start networking and recruiting students for a tutoring service that would help the community. Why waste more than twenty-eight years of experience? My sister is sitting on top of a golden opportunity. You could also be sitting on a golden opportunity to generate income for yourself and your family. Stop for one moment and analyze your life skills. Can they be used to generate income that will assist you in meeting your monthly expenses? Only you can uncover your real income potential.

Plan of Action

List the things you currently like to do that could generate extra income.

_____

_____

_____

_____

_____

_____

_____

_____

_____

_____

_____

_____

_____

_____

_____

Perception of People and Their Decision-Making Abilities

As I stated in previous chapters, something happens to our perception of people when they age past fifty. Fifty appears to be the magical age that we believe to be old. Perception is a process by which individuals organize and interpret sensory impressions in order to give meaning to their environment. However, what we perceive can be substantially different from objective reality. What if we know someone that is fifty years of age but looks thirty; is he or she labeled as old?

If we as a society believe that individuals over fifty are not employable or useful, how are they going to generate income as they age? Three factors are usually involved in determining how we perceive things; factors include the perceiver, the target, and situation.

- Perceiver. When you look at a target and attempt to interpret what you see, your interpretation is heavily influenced by your personal characteristics, your attitudes, personality, motives, interests, past experiences, and expectations.

For instance, if you expect police officers to be authoritative or young people to be lazy, you may perceive them as such regardless of their actual traits.

- Target. Characteristics of the target also affect what we perceive. Loud people are more likely to be noticed in a group than quiet ones. So too are extremely attractive or unattractive individuals. Because we do not look at targets in isolation, the relationship of a target to its background also influences perception, as does our tendency to group close things and similar things together.

- Situation. The time at which we see an object or event can influence our attention, as can location, light, or any number of situational factors. At a nightclub on Saturday night, you may not notice a guest dressed elegantly. Yet that same person's attire for your Monday-morning management class would certainly catch your attention. Neither the perceiver nor the target has changed between Saturday night and Monday morning, but the situation is different.

How can a person change his or her perception of older workers? What determines or sets our perception of older workers? Two concepts that have a great impact on our perceptions are the halo effect and stereotyping. With the halo effect we draw a general impression about an individual on the basis of single characteristics, such as intelligence, sociability, or appearance. The reality of the halo effect was confirmed in a classic study in which subjects were given a list of traits such as intelligent, skillful, and practical, industrious, and warm (The Halo Effect, 2008). They were asked to evaluate the person to whom those traits applied. Subjects judged the person to be wise, humorous, popular, and imaginative. When the same list was modified to include "cold" instead of "warm," a completely different picture emerged. Clearly, the subjects were allowing a single trait to influence their overall impression of the person they were judging. What part would attitude and vision play in our perception of others?

Would we consider perception of another bad or good? I guess it would depend on our attitude. A bad attitude can have a negative effect on our vision. Never doubt your vision because of your background or education. Just because you faced struggles or don't have the best education, never think your vision is not as important as anyone else's. If you see the world as a happy, loving place, then that is where you are going to live. But if you see the world as a destructive, negative, and dangerous place, then that will be your reality. A positive attitude can help you impact your vision, and vision can help you achieve life's goals.

Steps Taken

List the steps you are going to take to change your perceptions about workers that are in their fifties.

_____

_____

_____

_____

_____

_____

_____

_____

_____

_____

_____

_____

_____

_____

Searching for Employment

If you have read this book and believe that you want to find an employer instead of being unemployed, there are several steps you should take. The first thing you must do is summarize all of your experiences and education in presentation format. Practice presenting this information to an audience with either family members or friends to critique your presentation. How does your presentation appear to others?

Discussing and presenting your skills will help you gain confidence in your abilities. Selling your skills to an employer is 80 percent of an interview. A person must be able to sell his or her skills to an employer. Selling yourself is similar to selling your car to a friend. You need to make a good first impression to sell your personal assets to a company.

Once you have mastered your presentation summary, it is time to develop answers to interview questions, another area where you need to set yourself apart from the pack. The most common interview questions are as follows: what are your strengths, what are your weaknesses, why are you interested in working for our company, where do you see yourself in five or ten years, why do you want to leave your current company, tell us about a time you made a mistake, discuss your educational background, why should we hire you? These are just basic questions that probably will be asked during an interview. Practice your answers!

With years of experience working, identifying transferable skills that an employer can use should be an easy task. Ask yourself questions like, "What are your three favorite accomplishments?" What activities make you the happiest?" This will help you find your transferable skills. Also, apply transferable skills to your résumé; organize your résumé by skill area chronologically or functionally. Categorize all applicable skills, highlight experiences, and group them in categories such as professional or personal.

Workers Over Fifty Are the New Unemployable?

I read an article recently that stated that people over fifty are too young to retire. They may also be too old to get hired. Also mentioned was the fact that older workers were less likely to lose their jobs during a recession, but those who were laid off are facing tougher conditions than their younger colleagues. It was determined that workers in their fifties were 20 percent less likely than workers aged twenty-five to fifty-four to become re-employed. Older workers also experience the longest bouts of unemployment.

Unemployment in general, and long-term unemployment in particular, affects the financial and emotional well-being of individuals, their families, and their friends. Workers of all ages who lost jobs during the Great Recession indicated that their financial situations were precarious and that they utilized a range of strategies to cope with their circumstances, from tapping into savings to increasing credit card debt to going to emergency food pantries. Those nearing traditional retirement age may not have the time to recover financially from the blow of late career job loss. A relatively weak safety net means that many of these unemployed workers are not eligible for unemployment insurance, and they lack money for health insurance. Understandably, the older unemployed worker will experience high levels of anxiety, depression, and stress.

It appears the older worker has to find ways to survive. It was determined that financial hardships for older workers required them to use retirement accounts and savings accounts. They also will have limited availability of unemployment insurance, a lack of health care benefits, especially for those not old enough for Medicare, and the struggle to find ways to survive while seeking new employment.

The American worker might as well get familiar with being unemployed and unemployable by the time they reach age forty. Forget fifty; corporate America considers workers old at age forty, the actual age at which an employee becomes a burden. It is not like the good old days when an employer valued older employees and valued longevity, knowledge, and seniority. Times have changed and employers' attitudes have changed. The new economy is not bad only for older workers; it is also terrible for newer workers.

Getting old, getting sick, getting hurt, doing the wrong thing outside of work, wrong politics, etc. will get you fired! Getting old is now the worst thing you can do. Because there is no longer any career path and no loyalty, what are employees going to do when they get old?

Plan of Action

Describe your plan to prevent being part of the new unemployable.

_____

_____

_____

_____

_____

_____

_____

_____

_____

_____

_____

_____

_____

Become a Tutor

If someone wanted to become a tutor, what should he or she do? During my research I discovered ten things:

1. Identify your expertise. No doubt you already know what that is, but if not, or if your expertise is broad, focus on a favorite discipline or topic.
2. Gain recognition. It helps to attain recognition of your qualifications by being actively involved in the knowledge or discipline you are representing.
3. Consult an attorney. If you want to tutor school children, there will likely be local rules and laws concerning this.
4. Understand the curriculum. Make sure you know and understand the curriculum you are going to teach.
5. Make your lessons interesting and interactive. With good lessons students will do much of the work; you will guide them to discovery.
6. Listen to your students; respond to what they know or don't understand, and prepare future lessons to account for any deficiencies.
7. Put your name out there. Becoming a private

tutor can be very rewarding, especially if you are an expert in a demanding field.

8. Talk to teachers who teach you in the subject you are planning to tutor, ask them to tell students who need help.
9. Advertise. Send fliers and announcements, newspaper ads, etc.
10. Talk to people you know. Speak with your friends, parents, or siblings about your tutoring services, and offer them a discount if they refer their friends.

All tutors must bear in mind that their tutoring should never dominate the lesson; that demotivates the learner, causing him or her to lose interest in the task altogether. This problem generally occurs when the tutor attempts to exercise control over a task that is within the learner's ability to perform. Another potential problem faced by tutors is trying to teach a skill to someone who is not interested in learning, or teaching a subject that may not be familiar with.

Remember, the definition of a tutor is a person who gives individuals, or in some cases small groups, instruction. The purpose of tutoring is to help students help themselves or to assist or guide them to the point at which they become an independent learner and thus no longer need a tutor. The ultimate purpose of tutoring is to create independent learners. Tutors should, essentially, work themselves out of a job, at least with individual tutees.

Plan of Action

List the steps you are going to take to become a tutor.

_____

_____

_____

_____

_____

_____

_____

_____

_____

_____

_____

_____

_____

_____

_____

_____

Entrepreneurial Opportunity

What happens to the information technology employees that are laid off after twenty-five years? Let's analyze the position and years of hands-on experience, years of training, seminars, and teaching others how to comprehend some sort of technology, years of working with others trying to solve problems.

To become a successful entrepreneur or consultant three things are really important. 1) You need to be really good at something, have real expertise in an industry, sector, or business discipline, and have good interpersonal skills, or you won't get initial clients. You need to be able to apply that expertise and knowledge in a setting other than that of your previous employer, whether you have come from the public or private sector. Also, you must be able to think in a structured and objective manner, be good at problem solving, have the ability to write proposals that clients will be prepared to read and act upon, and be able to manage your team and projects. 2) You have to be exceptionally good at selling and marketing—selling yourself, selling your ideas, selling your pricing, selling your methodologies. You may be good at what you do, but are you going to get the contract? You have the courage to ask for the order, learn how to close the deal, and be comfortable networking and looking for business. 3) You have to be good at building relationships with clients, and understanding your accountability to them, or you won't get any the first time or any time after that. Just get into consulting, start your own firm, become a freelance or contract consultant, or become a portfolio worker. Portfolio workers work for a variety of companies concurrently. As you have already noticed, this description sounds like a training ground for a consultant or entrepreneur.

The basic definition of an entrepreneur is someone who exercises initiative by organizing a venture to take benefit of an opportunity and, as the decision maker, decides what, how, and how much of a good or service will be produced. The basic definition of a consultant is an expert at recognizing problems and shaping solutions to those problems. The need for problem solvers among large and small businesses worldwide has been greater. The ever-changing moods of the buyer plus the myriad of crisis situations that business people face almost daily have created a market for the alert consultant.

Plan of Action

List the steps you are going to take to become a consultant or an entrepreneur.

_____

_____

_____

_____

_____

_____

_____

_____

_____

_____

_____

_____

_____

Past Motivation

During my career with GM, I was really focused on presentation; therefore, given any practice to present something, I took full advantage of the opportunity. I did not realize at the time how important presenting would be in my future work life; however, I always felt it was the best part of my job. Presenting ideas to coworkers—I loved the challenge. As I look back on my ability to communicate orally, with audiences of all ages, it is astounding to realize that public speaking is what most people fear. Most people would rather die than speak to an audience.

Motivating forces have always existed in our world. What motivates one person may be a DE motivator for others. What one person calls a de-motivator may be a motivator to others. I have witnessed acts of dramatic motivation throughout our society. I have seen brothers and sisters growing up in the same household with the same parents achieve the opposite of whatever their siblings accomplish. One sibling becomes CEO of a company, and the other becomes a below-average employee moving from company to company throughout life. How do we discern the true motivating forces within each individual?

If we analyze the term *motivation* more closely, we will discover that motivation is a continuous process that occurs in our brains on a daily basis. We are motivated throughout our day to accomplish tasks or complete activities. The chief motivator for every person lies within his or her thoughts. What we think about becomes a driving force in our total existence. Existence in what we do every day is determined by our thought process.

Your thoughts are like clouds passing through the sky, your field of awareness. Just noticing and letting go of your thoughts and thought process without judging or evaluating them can free you from the constraints of constant worry and analyzing.

Motiving Steps Taken

List the steps that appear to motivate you each day regarding generating income or finding employment.

_____

_____

_____

_____

_____

_____

_____

_____

_____

_____

_____

_____

_____

_____

_____

_____

_____

_____

_____

_____

_____

_____

_____

_____

_____

Summary

After reviewing this book and opening your mind to the concepts and theories discussed, it is time to develop your plan of action. Throughout this book we have talked about the endless opportunities that are presented to everyone every day. We have uncovered ways to become entrepreneurs or business owners doing jobs that you currently enjoy. Entrepreneurs and business owners see opportunities where everybody else sees problems, chaos, and confusion. It is their ability to envision a better tomorrow that guides them toward success. Successful entrepreneurs have the courage to do what most people would not, despite circumstances.

As you have noticed I am an advocate for people changing their lives. If you are over fifty years of age, eventually your employer will make you change your life, by layoff, firing, or job reassignment. Therefore, you should take action before being *forced* to take action. Having a plan enables you to build powerful, positive momentum in your efforts. Anything that is worth doing is also worth the time and effort spent to establish a workable plan. Plan to succeed and you will. Finding a job after fifty can be an easier process than society wants you to believe. Follow my steps and suggestions to determine what your next steps will be, to become a consultant, entrepreneur, or business owner. Remember, it is as simple as determining what your likes and dislikes are. Next, decide what you have experience doing. Finally, ensure that it is something that you enjoy. These steps will guarantee that you will have a job when you are fifty years of age and over.

References

American Psychological Association. Stress in America. Medical Humanities and Social Sciences, Florida State University College of Medicine, 2012.

DeVito, Joseph. *Interpersonal Communication.* 12th ed. New York: Pearson Education, 2009.

David, Watson. Division of Guilford Publications. New York, NY. Guilford Press, 2000.

Durbin, J. Andrew. *Essentials of Management.* Mason, OH: South – Western Cengage Learning, 2010.

Efraim Turban, King David. *Electronic Commerce.* New York: Pearson Education, 2011.

Johnson, Tony and Robyn, Spizman. *Will Work from Home.* New York: Berkley Publishing Group, 2008.

Kurtz, Annalyn. Workers over 50 Are the New Unemployable. *CNN Money.* February 26, 2013.

Maslow, Abraham. New York, NY. Edwin Mellen Press, 1991.

Merriam-Webster. - .com, retrieved May 8, 2011 from http//www.merriam-webster.com/dictionary 2011.

Monthly Labor Review. Bureau of Labor Statistics. United States. 2007.

Selkoe, Dennis. Brain Study. Center for Neuro-logic Diseases, 1992.

Silvus, Carol. *Job Hunting after 50.* Boston: Cengage Learning, 2012.

The Conference Board. Com, retrieved from – http// www.conference-board.org. 2013.

The Halo Effect .com, retrieved from http//www.the-halo-effect.com. 2008.

Wicker, Don. *Attitude Is # 1.* Bloomington, IN: AuthorHouse, 2010.

——. *Goal Setting: Confidence + Goals = Success.* Bloomington, IN: AuthorHouse, 2008.

——. *Job Satisfaction: Fact or Fiction.* Bloomington, IN: AuthorHouse, 2011.

——. *Motivation: An Interactive Guide.* Bloomington, IN: AuthorHouse, 2009.

——. *Success Is for Everyone.* Bloomington, IN: AuthorHouse, 2012.